This book is meant strictly for novelty purposes and is not to be used in place of real education. It is advised by the Author that you check the validity of the facts contained within this book.

THIS JUST IN!

Don't Forget...

- If it's a really smelly one, do a courtesy flush!
- Always check to make sure you're not out of toilet paper before you sit down to unload.
- If totally out of TP, you can use the pages of this book (please don't).
- Spray a little something when you're done.

Just The Facts

1

A group of flamingos is called
a "flamboyance."

2

Honey never spoils. Archaeologists have
found pots of honey in ancient Egyptian
tombs that are over 3,000 years old and
still edible.

3

The shortest war in history lasted
only 38-45 minutes, between Britain
and Zanzibar in 1896.

4

There are more stars in the
universe than grains of sand on
all the Earth's beaches.

5

A single strand of spaghetti is
called a "spaghetto."

Just The Facts

6

Octopuses have three hearts. 

7

The inventor of the Pringles can is now buried in one.

8

Bananas are berries, but strawberries aren't.

9

A "jiffy" is an actual unit of time, equal to 1/100th of a second.

10

Wombat poop is cube-shaped. 

Just The Facts

11   Cows have best friends and can become stressed when they are separated.

12   The Eiffel Tower can be 15 cm taller during the summer because of thermal expansion.

13   Pigeons can tell the difference between paintings by Monet and Picasso.

14   There's a town in Norway called "Hell," and it freezes over every winter.

15   Kangaroos can't walk backward.

Just The Facts

16

A group of porcupines is
called a "prickle."

17

A snail can sleep for three years.

18

The inventor of the frisbee was
turned into a frisbee after he died.

19

Hippos sweat a red substance
that acts as sunscreen and
antibiotic.

20

In Switzerland, it's illegal to
own just one guinea pig
because they get lonely.

Just The Facts

21 — Sea otters hold hands while sleeping to avoid drifting apart.

22 — The hashtag symbol is technically called an "octothorpe."

23 — The Twitter bird's official name is "Larry."

24 — Banging your head against a wall burns 150 calories an hour.

25 — Some cats are allergic to humans.

Just The Facts

26 The dot over the letter "i" is called a "tittle." 

27 A group of jellyfish is called a "smack." 

28 The inventor of the chocolate chip cookie sold the idea to Nestlé Toll House for a lifetime supply of chocolate.

29  You can't hum while holding your nose.

30 A group of bunnies is called a "fluffle."

Just The Facts

31

Scotland's national animal is the unicorn.

32

A "buttload" is an actual unit of measurement equal to 126 gallons.

33

Sloths can hold their breath longer than dolphins can.

34

The inventor of the Rubik's Cube took one month to solve the puzzle after creating it.

35

Dragonflies have been on Earth for over 300 million years.

Just The Facts

36

Turtles can breathe through their butts.

37

A group of ferrets is called a "business."

38

There are more fake flamingos in the world than real ones.

39

The shortest commercial flight in the world is just 57 seconds long, between two Scottish islands.

40

The longest hiccuping spree lasted for 68 years.

Just The Facts

41

It's impossible to tickle yourself.

42

Cows moo with regional accents.

43

The first person to win two Nobel Prizes was Marie Curie.

44

A group of lemurs is called a "conspiracy."

45

Giraffes have the same number of neck vertebrae as humans: seven.

Just The Facts

46

Elephants can't jump.

47

There's a species of jellyfish that is immortal.

48

A cat has been the mayor of an Alaskan town for 20 years.

49

Koalas have fingerprints almost identical to human fingerprints.

50

The world's largest snowflake on record measured 15 inches wide and 8 inches thick.

Just The Facts

51

Blue whales are the largest animals ever known to have lived on Earth.

52

The average person will spend six months of their life waiting for red lights to turn green.

53

The inventor of the microwave appliance only received $2 for his discovery.

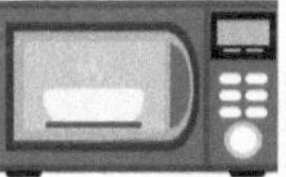

54

The heart of a shrimp is located in its head.

55

A group of giraffes is called a "tower."

Just The Facts

56

The cigarette lighter was invented before the match.

57

There are more lifeforms living on your skin than there are people on the planet.

58

Alaska is one-fifth the size of the entire United States and can fit the state of Rhode Island into it 425 times.

59

A bolt of lightning contains enough energy to toast 100,000 slices of bread.

60

The longest recorded flight of a chicken is 13 seconds.

Just The Facts

61 The world's termites outweigh the world's humans about 10 to 1.

62 If you lift a kangaroo's tail off the ground, it can't hop.

63 There are more public libraries in the United States than McDonald's.

64 A crocodile cannot stick its tongue out.

65 The world's oldest piece of chewing gum is over 9,000 years old.

Just The Facts

66

The Hawaiian alphabet has only 12 letters.

67

A duck's quack doesn't echo, and no one knows why.

68

Most lipstick contains fish scales.

69

The world's largest grand piano was built by a 15-year-old in New Zealand.

70

Butterflies taste with their feet.

Just The Facts

71

An ostrich's eye is bigger than its brain.

72

Tigers have striped skin, not just striped fur.

73

The blood of a horseshoe crab is blue.

74

The human nose can remember 50,000 different scents.

75

The shortest complete sentence in the English language is "I am."

Just The Facts

76

Slugs have four noses.

77

The inventor of the telephone, Alexander Graham Bell, never called his mother or wife; they were both deaf.

78

A flea can jump up to 200 times its own height.

79

The average person walks the equivalent of three times around the world in a lifetime.

80

Apples float because 25% of their volume is air.

Just The Facts

81 A cat's whiskers are generally about the same width as its body.

82 The inventor of the Super Soaker water gun was a NASA scientist.

83 Blue eyes don't actually contain blue pigment. They are technically invisible. The blue color is just an optical illusion.

84  The first email was sent by Ray Tomlinson to himself in 1971.

85 Polar bears have black skin under their white fur. 

Just The Facts

86

Bananas are naturally slightly radioactive due to their potassium content.

87

Bees can make colored honey. In France, bees were found producing blue and green honey after eating remnants of M&M's candy.

88

A day on Venus is longer than a year on Venus. Venus takes about 243 Earth days to rotate once but only about 225 Earth days to orbit the Sun.

89

Cleopatra lived closer in time to the Moon landing than to the construction of the Great Pyramid of Giza.

90

An eagle can kill a young deer and fly away with it.

Just The Facts

91

Dragonflies can see in all directions at the same time.

92

The inventor of the slinky was inspired by a tension spring falling off a table and "walking" across the floor.

93

Sharks are older than trees. Sharks have existed for around 400 million years, while trees have been around for about 350 million years.

94

In ancient Rome, a special room called a "vomitorium" was available for diners to purge food during feasts.

95

The world's largest pumpkin weighed over 2,600 pounds.

Just The Facts

96

Otters have a pocket in their skin where they keep their favorite rock.

97

The inventor of the waffle iron did not originally intend it for making waffles; it was meant to be a shoe press.

98

The longest word in the English language without a vowel is "rhythms."

99

Starfish can regenerate their arms, and in some cases, an entirely new starfish can grow from a single arm.

100

Dolphins have names for each other and can call out to specific individuals.

NO SH*T?

Man Writes Book For Poops

Hi, I'm Brandon Wilson. Author of this book. I hope you liked it, and that everything came out okay. Be on the lookout for more to come!

Don't forget to flush!